THE JOURNEY *to the*
INNER CHAMBER

{ *the introduction* }
STUDY GUIDE FOR SMALL GROUPS

ROCKY FLEMING

Prayer Cottage Publications – Rogers, AR

Scripture taken from the New American Standard Bible ®
Copyright © The Lockman Foundation

Printed in the United States of America

Cover Photo: The Whirlpool Galaxy from the Hubble Telescope
NASA, ESA, S. Beckwith (STScI)
and The Hubble Heritage Team (STScI/AURA)

Mission: To encourage and influence individuals toward an abiding relationship with Jesus Christ, through a journey to spiritual intimacy.

Vision: To transform lives through The Journey, enabling them to be a positive influence to their world around them.

contents

INTRODUCTION

Before you begin your small group study of The Journey to the Inner Chamber (Inner Chamber), I would like to provide some important thoughts for you to consider. Let's start with why I wrote this book and what inspired me. To answer this question, I must say that the book was originally written to provide a creative story that would point to deeper truths. This concept is called "Allegory," and includes metaphors, which is another form of hidden truth using examples of people or illustrations. Therefore, the story you will read in this book is a creative way, using fictional characters and events, to convey some important truths found within the Bible about being a true disciple of Christ. I say the accounts and people are fictional, but the people and events in the book are borrowed from some of my own personal experiences, and people I have personally known or known of. This story can be best understood by applying the characters and events to your life, and then finding identification with things you can understand from a personal standpoint. Make no mistake in thinking that this book is simply an entertaining story with no deeper meaning. I did not write this book just to sell books or raise revenue for a ministry. On the contrary, the story I wrote is using the allegory and metaphors are packed with biblical truths, and its objective is to raise up disciples for Christ. You will discover these truths, if you carefully look for them.

The effort you should make in your small group study is to identify those biblical truths within Inner Chamber and apply them to where you are right now in your own life. If you will allow the story to speak to you this way, by getting into it as an observer or even by looking through the perspective of the story teller, you will identify where you are presently in your journey with Christ, and where you need to go to become the disciple you deep down long to be. But don't stop with simply identifying where you are in your journey. Just because you might identify your present location on the path with your journey with Christ, it will do you no good to just remain there. It would be similar to being diagnosed with cancer and knowing specifically where it is located and how it needs to be treated, but taking no steps to remove or cure it. Likewise, the next step after your book study of The Journey to the Inner Chamber is to move forward to a life change that will lead you to become the man or woman God wants you to be. Therefore, I believe the next step after the completion of this book study will be critical for you, which brings me to the reason I wrote the book you have just read. It is a group study called, The Journey.

The Journey is small group curriculum that involves a nine-month process that helps a follower of Christ discover an intimate, abid-ing relationship with Him. You will be invited to join a group to go through this process with some other believers who are pursuing the same goal. The Journey was inspired to me by the Lord in 2001, and was first introduced to seven Christian businessmen who were friends of mine. After our first group, which lasted almost a year, the process was more fully developed over the next several years so that it could be more easily transferred. From its beginning, the process has been written to help a believer move forward in his or her per-sonal walk with Christ, and to become the disciple that God wants to make of His child. The Journey to the Inner Chamber, was written in

2004 with the purpose that it be used for assimilating small groups of believers to go through The Journey. That objective and purpose has not changed. It has always been about making true disciples for Christ. This is why I say the next step you take when you complete the book review will be critical.

I am providing some comments that our leaders have heard from men and women from all over the world as examples of how the hidden truths within Inner Chamber have stirred them to take the next step after reading the book.

"When I read Inner Chamber, I discovered that I really didn't know Christ. I had been raised in church, but didn't know that I had no true relationship with Jesus, but rather I had a religious idea about Him. The book showed me what a true relationship with Christ looks like and how to have it."

"I had struggled for years with my purpose and identity as a Christian. Inner Chamber helped me identify why I was struggling, and how to change it."

"I had no idea about what true Christian influence is. I thought it was dependent on prominence or power or prestige. Then I read about a character named Gabe, and I saw that those things our culture teaches us about influence are irrelevant for making a true impact on my world around me."

"I think all men ask the question of whether our life will make any difference in this world. I know I did. I now understand what Jesus meant when He said He wanted me to bear a fruit that lasts. He was talking about leaving a spiritual legacy that would follow after me. The Journey to the Inner Chamber and The Journey that followed have shown me how to allow Christ to create that legacy with my life."

"There is so much biblical truth in Inner Chamber. You just have to look for it in the story. I like discovering biblical truths this way. I went to church all my life and had somehow tuned out and missed these truths, even though they were being taught. The little book and our discussions helped me take the truths in the Bible from my brain to my heart, and I began to understand how God was speaking directly to me about the next steps I should take in becoming His disciple. The discipleship process that I participated in afterwards helped me find the personal transformation I was looking for."

Perhaps you can identify with one or two of these comments. I pray that you will discover answers for that "something" that is stirring deep down inside of you. God bless you as you read and discuss The Journey to the Inner Chamber.

Rocky

DISCUSSION GUIDE

GROUP DYNAMICS AND DISCUSSION PROCEDURES:
If your group is less than six people, a discussion facilitator is not necessary, for the discussion attendees can manage the discussion by simply reading the question and reacting to it by sharing their thoughts. Simply read the questions and discuss them amongst yourselves. Each question and answer will create group insights, and these insights will likely lead to a sub-question or personal application by group members. This is a fun and productive way for truths to be hammered home, provided one person doesn't dominate or feel led to "teach" the group. So allow the discussion to expand beyond the initial question. By allowing a free flowing discussion while staying close to the original question, you will discover a joyful benefit as you watch how the Holy Spirit teaches a group. But, stay close to the original question and thought in order to stay focused on the next steps in the process. That is the only critical concern with allowing this kind of flexibility in a discussion. Members in the group should be willing to monitor this concern and speak up if the discussion is headed away from the subject.

For larger groups, it is recommended that a group discussion facilitator be used so that discussions can stay on track. That is the primary purpose for a discussion facilitator. His or her role will be to facilitate discussion, but not teach it. This is essential to remember for good group dynamics, and so that each group member can personally uncover hidden truths. You will read the words "Self-Feeding" in the story. This would be a case in point where the application of that term is being applied, as a discussion leader allows a group member to "self-feed" with personal discovery rather than being spoon-fed by teaching insights of another person.

BIBLICAL INSIGHT: It is very important for your group to understand the scriptural and theological basis for The Journey to the Inner Chamber. Questions are provided to stimulate your discussion. It is recommended that your discussions unfold with the story. For instance, try to stay with the questions provided for Part 1 in the story before moving to Part 2. In addition, when a certain discussion point comes up, make sure you do not leave that point without looking at the theology. The scripture references that are provided will help.

ASK FOR THE SPIRIT'S LEADERSHIP: We believe prayer and dependence on the Holy Spirit's presence and leadership is essential to a good discussion where truth is both discovered and applied to a life. Your effort as a group or as a discussion facilitator is to create a climate where a grace driven, joyful discovery process is able to thrive. By doing so, biblical truth, which is often overlooked or not understood, will be uncovered and applied to a life. This process will lead to life change as steps toward true discipleship are taken.

LENGTH OF EACH SESSION: Although your time and form may vary in each group, this study is written to be used by a small group on a weekly basis for six weeks. You should allocate ninety minutes for each group, as good discussion will eat up the time. You can shoot for a sixty-minute gathering. But don't be surprised if you need more time.

SIX WEEKS—TWO PARTS—SIX SESSIONS: The Journey to the Inner Chamber is presented in two parts. Each session will build a foundation for the truths found in the next session. If your group wants to linger longer in a particular session, let them. This lingering time is often the work of the Spirit. So let Him lead you. That is the climate you are praying for. If your group goes longer than the designed six weeks, it will likely be because truth is really being discovered and absorbed. This is good.

God bless you as you proceed through the study of The Journey to the Inner Chamber.

PART ONE

SESSION ONE

THE REFUGEE CAMP

(COVERS JOURNEY BOOK CHAPTERS 2-3)

Start by reading Romans 8:19-23. After you read this passage, discuss among yourselves how and why God's creation is subjected to "futility." The Amplified Bible calls it, "condemned to frustration." Why would God allow this? What is He hoping will happen?

Question: The Refugee Camp is presented as The World hidden from our view. Call it the spirit world and the inner condition of man if you like. What do you see in the point of view presented in the book that is not seen by most people? Discuss your thoughts and answers to the questions below:

THE PROBLEM:

- **Starving people**. What are the people starving for? (Discuss)

- **Who do these starving people represent?** Does this sound like the people mentioned in the passage in Romans 8:19-23? (Discuss)

- **How did this condition originate?** Read the quote from Inner Chamber and discuss the following questions:

  "Messenger," I asked, "What caused this starving condition in mankind?" He answered, "Because the father and mother of mankind chose to disobey the Creator while in the paradise He created for them, the process of spiritual starvation began. The sin of mankind's parents created a separation from the Creator, for themselves and all their children. However, in His mercy and grace, God created a way for mankind to come back to Him. It is the only solution for Mankind's redemption and survival. That solution, and it alone, brings mankind back to the Creator."

- **Is there hope for these people?** In Romans 8:19-23 passage, you read about a hope that emerges from the futility and frustration in the world. What do you think it is? (Discuss)

The Culprit and his counterfeits

Read the following quote from Inner Chamber and discuss the questions that follow:

"Sir," I asked with exasperation, "Why don't they just go back to God? All they have to do is look around and see the condition they are in."

"The great Deceiver convinces them that there is no problem his remedies can't fix. He dulls them with earthly treasures. He makes them feel special by appealing to their pride. He appears as an angel of light and convinces them that all they need is what he offers. A little more money or a new job or a new love in their life or the applause of man—these are some of his misleading strategies. But what he is really doing is

leading them to the fire that will eventually consume them along with him. Think of your world, and you will remember the counterfeits that keep people from seeing the truth and trusting God's provision. Think of your own life and the counterfeits you had to overcome."

• **Counterfeits:** What are some counterfeit pleasures and treasures that you see that make someone dull to their inner man needs? Do you see any counterfeits in your own life that you are buying into? (Discuss)

• **The Masks:** How do the man-made conditions of success and prosperity mask or hide the true inner condition of a man or woman? Do these temporary conditions or counterfeits really satisfy the groans and labors mentioned in Romans that all people have? When does the mask come off? Does it come off after the loss of the false security we have? Does it come off when we are honest with our personal, inner need? Does it come off after the frustration and futility of failure? Does it finally come off when we face death? (Discuss)

Godly Influence
RESCUE BY INFLUENCE:

Read the following quote and discuss the questions that follow:

One of the riders dismounted and went directly to a starving human who was slumped near me. The rider said something I couldn't hear. The starving man nodded weakly. Then the rider removed a flask of water that had been strapped to his side. He gently lifted the man's head and let him drink. Next the rider opened a bag and took fruit and bread from it. He again assisted the starving human by lifting his head while he ate. All the while the rider stroked the human's back and offered comfort. The human gained enough strength from the nourishment to stand. At this point the rider lifted the once starving man to the back of his noble steed and mounted it with him. The rider held his shield over the human to protect him from the flaming arrows. As they rode toward the castle, the rider continued to share his food and water with the human as he protected him from the arrows.

- **The Influence of Providing:** How does serving another person at their point of need, only if it is meeting a basic need, communicate the love of Christ? If we are able, does being generous in meeting the basic needs of people offer influence to our world around us? Did Jesus do this? Does He do it for you now? (Discuss)

- **The Influence of Caring**: In the scene above, we see a powerful knight, called Influencer, offer compassion as he stroked the starving man's back. Was the food the only thing needed by the starving man? Why do you think showing compassion helped this man in a deeper area of need? Will compassion to the hurting person influence your world around you? Did Jesus do this? Does He do it for you now? (Discuss)

- **The Influence of Protection:** In the scene above, we see Influencer protect the refugee from the flaming arrows. He did this with his shield. Read Ephesians 6:10-18. Look at the weapons listed in these verses for protection in spiritual warfare. In verse 16 we read about the "shield of faith." How did Influencer's shield of faith protect the weaker man? How does your faith serve to protect the weaker people in your life? Did Jesus do this? Does He do it for you now? (Discuss)

The Nature of the Battle

Read the following quote and discuss the spiritual warfare that surrounds you and discuss the questions that follow:

"What about those hideous creatures that are shooting flaming arrows at Influencer?" I asked.

Messenger answered, "They are soldiers of the great Deceiver, the enemy of the Lord and mankind. These creatures are doing their best to keep the humans in their miserable condition. They don't want the humans to be saved from the ultimate death and fire they will face. By shooting at Influencer, they are trying to wound or discourage him. But their arrows cannot get to him. As long as Influencer keeps partaking of the Feast in the Inner Chamber, he will be strong and resist their arrows. The armor that Influencer wears will stand against the flaming missiles and all other schemes of the Deceiver."

- Satan is called a liar and a deceiver and the Accuser in the Bible. How does he accuse Christians? What are ways that he deceives Christians? How does he deceive you?

- What are demons? How do they battle against believers? How can we stand against them? Read the following verses for assurance:

"Behold, I have given you authority to tread on serpents and scorpions, and over all the power of the enemy, and nothing shall hurt you." Luke 10:19 (ESV)

"Beloved, do not believe every spirit, but test the spirits to see whether they are from God, for many false prophets have gone out into the world." 1 John 4:1 (ESV)

"Do not be overcome by evil, but overcome evil with good."Romans 12:21(ESV)

The seventy-two returned with joy, saying, "Lord, even the demons are subject to us in your name!" Luke 10:17 (ESV)

He who dwells in the shelter of the Most High will abide in the shadow of the Almighty. I will say to the Lord, "My refuge and my fortress, my God, in whom I trust." For he will deliver you from the snare of the fowler and from the deadly pestilence. He will cover you with his pinions, and under his wings you will find refuge; his faithfulness is a shield and buckler. Psalms 91:1-4 (ESV)

- How do the verses above provide you assurance that you too will be protected by God if you will become an Influencer to your world around you? Consider this question and close your session with prayer.

SESSION TWO

THE BRIDGE

(COVERS JOURNEY BOOK CHAPTERS 4-5)

Religions—a false sense of hope
To the Kingdom

Read the following excerpt from the book to get a sense of how false religions can steal our appetite for a true relationship with God through Jesus Christ. It is a tactic from the enemy of mankind to redirect the natural desire mankind has to have a restored relationship with our Creator.

As we moved forward, I noticed a throng of starving humans eating at tables outside the castle walls. Influencer paid no attention to the activity, but I noticed that Refugee was looking longingly at the food that was being passed out. Refugee began to point to the food and motioned to Influencer that he wanted to go to it.

I saw Influencer stop, turn to Refugee and speak to him while motioning to the food. After a moment, Refugee nodded as if he understood what Influencer was saying, and they continued their journey. I had to ask, for I couldn't understand why Influencer wouldn't let Refugee eat when food was obviously available.

"Look closely at what is being offered. Also look at the results. You will see one of the great deceptions that the Deceiver gives to mankind," he responded.

I eased through the crowd and looked at the food. There was nothing of substance. It looked like many of the appetizers I had seen at parties. They were fun, interesting and different looking but lacked nutritional value. I looked closely at the people who were fighting for the dainty items. I wanted to see whether the appetizers made any difference, but I saw no change in their starving appearance. They were still the same pitiful-looking wretches who were destined for death and fire. They were still dying of malnutrition. But most of them had lost their hunger pangs and their raging appetites had abated. Again, I needed to ask the meaning of what I saw.

"What is being offered has no substance and the starving humans are not saved from their destiny of death and fire. Can you tell me what else this means?" I asked.

"Think of your world," Messenger answered. "What you are seeing is a representation of one of the great deceptions of your age. The great Deceiver has established different religions for mankind that are designed to take away mankind's hunger for the Father. The appetizers represent these religions. The Deceiver knows that mankind is starving for a restored relationship with the Lord. Therefore, he has created counterfeits that will divert the people by giving them a false enlightenment. They think that when they

partake of these religions they know Him and have a right relationship with Him, but they have been led astray. I call these humans Religion Victims." (see Isaiah 29:13 and Deuteronomy 12:29-32)

Now think of your world

- How do you think the false religions dull someone in their pursuit and understanding of how to have a real relationship with God through Jesus? (Discuss)

- Have any of you had experiences with a false religion or a false prophet? (Discuss)

- Do you know any "religion victims?" How did their religion change them? (Discuss)

- What are some things that appear appealing in these religions? Rules? Formulas? Acceptance (which is a big aspect of a cult)? Charismatic leader? Etc. (Discuss)

- Why do you think these religions fail to provide what they promise? (Discuss)

False Religions Continued

Continue reading about false religions from the following excerpt.

Messenger continued, "A Religion Victim is a seeker who is looking and sampling on the periphery of knowing God. These people try a lot of religions in hopes of finding Him. They try everything from legalism to Buddhism. They try Eastern Mysticism to Transcendentalism. You name the 'ism,' and they try it. They just won't take the simple truth of God's provision, which allows them to come to Him, for they are deceived in thinking there is, something else. I tell you, any pursuit of God that does not come through His provision alone will not find Him. There is only one path to God and that is through His Son, Jesus Christ."

"What is most distressing is that there are some churches in this group that are called by Jesus' name. But they teach that there are other ways to God and that Jesus is only one of many. I tell you, teachers of this false doctrine will be dealt with most severely on Judgment Day. Know this: Jesus Christ, God's only provision for mankind, will never be found in the appetizer section with other religions."

Messenger continued. "Christianity should never be identified as a religion, for what is offered is a right relationship with God through His grace. It is not a result of mankind's works or religious behavior. I detest it when people call God's provision 'religion'!"

I thought Messenger was finished, but it was obvious that he was highly agitated over the religion thing. So he continued. "What do religions bring that is so appetizing? Legalistic rules that give a false sense of security? Programs that attempt to box God in by trying to make Him something they can understand, rather than considering that He is unimaginable and inestimable? What about the self-actualization religions? All they do is feed their ego needs. Make no mistake: To a hungry person these 'appetizer religions' look good and do what the Deceiver designed them to do. They will keep people from the real thing, the real feast that is found in a personal, intimate relationship with God through His Son, Jesus Christ and they must be avoided."

Please read: The word religion covers a broad spectrum of religious beliefs and practices, as is mentioned in the excerpt. What is the fundamental problem? At the heart of most religions is a desire to be loved and accepted by God. This is a basic core need of mankind. Therefore, it becomes an effort of a false religion to teach that we earn God's love and acceptance because of our religious devotion, or activity, or dedication, or attention to becoming attentive to a deeper commitment to the beliefs of the false religion. In other words, they teach that it is man's dedicated effort to get to God by what is done by man, and God's love and acceptance must be earned. Christianity, on the other hand, is God's effort to get to mankind through what He has done. It is the work of Jesus on the cross that opened the way for us to God and His acceptance. It is by His grace, through faith that we are saved, not as a result of the works of man. God's love is now available through Jesus Christ and Christianity acknowledges, believes and accepts what Christ has done to provide this relationship with God that is offered. This is the core difference in a religion that seeks God and the relationship in Christianity that takes us into God's heart.

After Reading Ephesians 2:8, discuss the following questions:

1. How does God's grace open the door to a relationship with Him? (Grace means God's free and unconditional love and favor.) (Discuss)

2. How does our faith in what Jesus did for us help walk us into that open door? (Discuss)

3. Is it the decision made for us by a church or family or tradition that brings us into the family of God, or is it a decision that we must all make individually? Read John 1:11-13. (Discuss)

4. If religion is defined as man's effort to seek God and be accepted by Him, then Christianity must be defined as a relationship with God. How does knowing that you have a relationship with God as a Father, help you understand how false religions are not the answer for the deep need that mankind has to be restored to our Creator? (Discuss)

The Atonement of Christ—True Hope

Read the following excerpt from the book to understand the spiritual transition from death to life that occurs when we accept the Atonement of God through our belief and acceptance of Jesus Christ. Refugee asking to be admitted into God's Kingdom represents this. The Bridge that he crosses represents Jesus Christ. Jesus is our "bridge" crossing the impossible separation that exists between sinful man and Holy God. Note that after Refugee crosses the Bridge, the maturity of this transformed life does not occur immediately, which is the challenge most Christians face. At this point, we see only a "baby in Christ" being born. The process after his decision will either lead to his maturity as a believer, or he will remain retarded in his spiritual growth and fail to become the man God intends for him to be.

The Bridge

(Messenger) "The great Deceiver has much of mankind convinced that good works and religion can cross the moat and scale the walls to God's kingdom. They cannot. There is no good work that mankind can do, nor any religion that can conquer this separation. There is only one way to enter His Kingdom and that is over the Bridge that God established. The Bridge that Refugee just crossed represents God's provision for mankind, which is His Son, Jesus Christ. He is

the way, the truth and the life, and no one can come to God in any other way. Mankind must come through Him alone. Jesus is the Bridge from God to mankind. Jesus laid down His life for mankind in obedience to the Father so that whoever would believe this and come to God through this belief would be saved from death and fire."

"The decision to cross the Bridge had to be made by Refugee alone. Influencer had explained the process to Refugee. He walked Refugee all the way to a point of decision, but it was Refugee's choice to make. Coming to God cannot be attained through parents, friends or well-wishers. A person may grow up in church and have a family legacy of belief in Jesus, but the decision is still up to him. The Father has no grandchildren, only children. This is the reason you saw Influencer step away from Refugee when the time came for the decision. It was between Refugee and God."

"Refugee recognized the gift that was being offered to him through God's provision. Influencer had done a good job, by his life's example, of getting the point across to Refugee. But the decision was now in Refugee's hands, and he made his decision. When Refugee prayed to the Lord, he said he recognized that he was a sinner and was lost. He said he was aware that he didn't deserve His love or the salvation that was being offered. He was tired of the life he was living and wanted to give it to God to do with as He saw fit. Refugee said he wanted to receive the provision that had been made for him and become God's child. At that point, the Bridge was lowered and you saw what happened." (see John 14:6, John 10:9 and Romans 5:1-2)

After you have read the above excerpt, discuss the following questions:

1. Have you ever been confused about the process of becoming a Christian? What are some common misunderstandings that have confused you? (Discuss)

2. Why do you think God would require a well-thought-out decision to accept His offer of a relationship with Him, rather than a blanket coverage of forgiveness for everyone? (Consider that God created mankind in His own image which would also give us the God given right to accept or reject His plan for us, as Adam and Eve did.) (Discuss)

3. If you were to die tonight, would you be certain, without a doubt that you have "crossed the Bridge" and have a saving relationship with Jesus Christ? If not, you no longer have to live with this doubt. Now is the time to accept the gift of salvation and the relationship that God the Father wants you to have with Him. (Please pray about this individually and if you need further guidance or information, ask a mature believer or a pastor of a solid church what your next step should be.)

Close your session in prayer, and be sure to ask the Lord to reveal Himself to any who desire to walk across "The Bridge".

SESSION THREE

BEYOND THE BRIDGE

(COVERS JOURNEY BOOK CHAPTERS 6-9)

The Table of Sweets

As we proceed into the Kingdom, we need to understand what is represented. Note: Although a transformation into an eternal life begins after Refugee crossed the Bridge, his maturity is not immediate. It requires spiritual nutrition to build spiritual muscles and to become mature. The fact is, like most new converts, Refugee (now Learner) was still weak and vulnerable to the voice that lures him back to old habits and the counterfeits in his old life. So he needs nurturing and strengthening from the spiritual food he finds in the Kingdom. But, not all food in the Kingdom will grow a believer into maturity. An example, an insufficient food was found immediately when he entered the Kingdom. He was greeted with the Table of Sweets. Read the following excerpt from the book and discuss why this diet will not satisfy, nor will it mature a new convert.

I began to look around the courtyard. We were not yet in the castle but were within the Kingdom of God. As Influencer and Learner walked arm in arm toward the castle, I noticed a scene similar to what had occurred outside. There were tables with food. Standing around the tables were former refugees in their gleaming white robes. They were eating something, but I noticed that the refugees had changed only slightly in appearance.

Although they didn't look like walking death anymore, they still looked frail, sickly and vulnerable to disease. Learner said something to Influencer. I could tell that Learner wanted to dig into what was being offered, but Influencer stopped and explained something. Learner nodded, and he and Influencer kept moving toward the castle. I asked, "Messenger, what I am seeing here? Why couldn't Learner eat at this place?" Messenger responded, "You have seen Learner come across the Bridge and enter into a relationship with God. He did that when he accepted God's provision. But he still has a long way to go before he is the mature spiritual man he needs to be. The maturity I speak of requires real spiritual food. Influencer explained this to him and told him that this is not the place to stop if he wants to mature and become spiritually healthy. You will note that other former refugees stopped to eat. Look at what they are eating and you will understand better why they are not getting as healthy as they should." I moved toward the table, which was full of various kinds of sweets. They were attractive and tasty but offered little nutrition. It was little wonder that the refugees eating here were not getting stronger and still looked frail. "What does this represent?" I asked. Messenger replied, "In your world, some churches have forgotten their mission to feed the flocks that have been entrusted to them, with the real food found in God's Word.

This food and the table represent those particular churches. "Those churches have diluted God's Word to make it acceptable to their congregations. For the most part, they have good hearts and intentions, but their message is laced with a worldly agenda and they no longer teach the total truth that was given to them for building up the Church. They have sweetened their message and watered it down to make it attractive and easily digested by the babies in their congregation. In doing so they are creating confusion and a mixed message. This is why many in their congregation think that right is wrong and wrong is right. These teachers don't want to offend but consequently they allow their flocks to wallow in ignorance and unrepentance. They offer an explanation that God's grace covers it all but the real reason they say this is because they are afraid to speak a truth that will divide the congregation."

"If they speak God's Word in total and in truth, it will divide darkness from light. But, if they do, God's children will grow strong and be made safe. If these churches do not speak the truth of God's Word and let it work its way into His children's hearts, these children will stay spiritually anemic and be susceptible to the flaming arrows in their everyday lives. A steady diet of sweet messages is the wrong diet for God's children, for this kind of food is not nutritious enough to grow them into mature believers."

To relate the problem with the Table of Sweets, we need to contrast it with what scripture says about it with regards to maturing a believer. Look what 2 Timothy 3:16 says:

"All Scripture is breathed out by God and profitable for teaching, for reproof, for correction, and for training in righteousness"

1. In the scripture above, we are given some important living instructions found in God's Word. First, God's wisdom is given to us from Him personally. Several people penned it over a period of about 1600 years, but God Himself inspired it. Next, we read that this inspired word of God teaches us to understand Him better, and, as well, how to live a better life, for it reproofs us, corrects us, and trains us to follow a right path. With this is mind, answer the following questions:

- If our life requires change to mature as a believer, and all people require this, do you think true reproof, instruction and training in righteousness would require an uncomfortable adjustment for most believers? Why or why not? (Discuss)

- Would an immature believer normally be willing to seek the hard-to-find hidden truths in God's word on his or her own, or do we need another mature and solid influence that would challenge us to look and seek the deeper truths? Why or why not? (Discuss)

- What are some examples that we see nowadays that would indicate that many churches and Christians are allowing the current social norms to change them rather than followers of Christ changing their culture? How could following God's inspired word challenge, but also help these believers know the difference?

The Banquet Table

In the book, because of the wisdom of Influencer, Learner was guided to look for a better source than the diluted teachings of the **Table of Sweets** to find what he needed to mature as spiritual man. He was led to the **Banquet Table** where a team of gifted people

within the Kingdom who were raised up by God to help him mature
was waiting. At the heart of this place was the food of God's word
that was fed to him just as a baby would be fed until he could
become a **Self-Feeder**. Read the following excerpt for a brief
synopsis of what was being communicated and discuss the questions
that follow:

*"Tell me what you have learned so far in this vision," he
(Messenger) said.*

*"Messenger, I realize that this vision is metaphorical for
what is happening in my world and the spiritual warfare that
is being waged for the soul of mankind. I also realize that
God reaches to mankind using believers empowered by the
Holy Spirit and the gospel message of God's provision for
mankind. I realize that God's provision for mankind is found
only through Jesus Christ and the sacrifice He made for us,
even though the enemy of our souls would try to convince us
otherwise. I realize that once someone comes to God through
Jesus Christ, he becomes God's child and it is His purpose
and plan to grow the believer to maturity. I realize that God
has given His children spiritual gifts to help build His family
into maturity. I realize the food that feeds our souls and
matures us is God's Word and prayer. Simply put, His Word
teaches us how to live."*

*Before I could continue, Messenger interrupted. "Now tell
me what the banquet table represents."*

*I answered, "I see that a new believer needs to first be taught
from God's Word very gently with the basics by someone who
can communicate these truths effectively. I also see that the
objective of this teacher should be to increase the new
believer's diet of the Word so that he can mature as a result*

of the deeper and hidden truths that are in God's Word."

Messenger stopped me to emphasize the point with his next question. "And what about the self-feeding?" Messenger asked.

"I see that this is the ultimate objective for the believer," I answered.

"Well, it's not the ultimate objective, but you can't get there without going through this level of growth," he said.

"You're talking about the Feast in the Inner Chamber again, aren't you?" I asked. "You're learning," he replied with a smile.

Discuss the following questions:

1. As we look at the people serving the new believer (Learner) what comes to your mind as examples of people who have served you and helped you either come to know Christ or grow as a believer? (Discuss)

2. In the following verse, we are given the theology behind the metaphor you have just read:

> *"Rather, speaking the truth in love, we are to grow up in every way into him who is the head, into Christ, from whom the whole body, joined and held together by every joint with which it is equipped, when each part is working properly, makes the body grow so that it builds itself up in love."*
> *Ephesians 4: 15-16 (ESV)*

3. Have you ever considered that there are actually other believers who have been gifted by God with certain spiritual gifts who can help you grow spiritually? How does it make you feel? (Discuss)

4. Have you ever considered that you also have been gifted with special gifts to serve others and once you have matured as a believer, you are a strategic part of God's work in His kingdom? Does that give you purpose and significance? (Discuss)

5. Have you ever considered that the Church is an organic "body" where Jesus Christ is the head, and each believer is a certain "body part?" Using this metaphor, how do you understand the Church should work together, and for what purpose? (Discuss)

The Exercise Room

I heeded messenger's instruction to watch Mentor and Learner. After one of Learner's meals, I saw Mentor instruct him to leave the table and go to a room off the banquet hall. I followed.

The room that Learner and Mentor entered was a large exercise room. It had all of the weights and equipment that could be found in the finest gyms. Mentor had Learner working on some light weights. Then he led Learner to a cot and instructed him to rest. After a while, Mentor took Learner back to the table to pray and be fed. He moved Learner closer to the heavier foods. After Learner ate, the cycle of training and resting would be repeated. Each time Learner entered the exercise room, greater weights were added to Learner's training regimen. This seemed confusing; if it related to spiritual growth in my world, I needed Messenger to clear it up. I asked that he help me understand the scene.

"You were at one time an athlete in your world, were you not?" He asked. I nodded, "Yes."

Messenger continued, "Well, think about your training. Were there not three main components for getting stronger and physically mature: nutrition, exercise and rest? What would it have been like if you participated in only one or two of the three? Nutrition without exercise would lead to fat. Rest without exercise would lead to laziness. Exercise without nutrition and rest would lead to physical breakdown. It is the same with spiritual growth.

"Again, I say, you are seeing a representation here in order to hammer home truth as it relates to a believer's spiritual growth in your world, so listen carefully."

I was all ears.

"The food in the banquet hall represents the nutritional value of God's Word to the believer," Messenger began. "The exercise room represents the trials and tests the believer will face. The resting cot represents the peace of God that follows the trials."

1. Can you relate to the value of nutrition, exercise and rest being the main components of strength and muscle development? How do you think these three components working together will help some-one grow physically?

2. How can someone grow spiritually using the same analogy, but using the components of scripture, trials and answered prayer?

3. What would spiritual growth look like?

Read the following excerpt from Inner Chamber and discuss the following questions.

"Messenger," I asked, "is it really necessary to go through these trials in order to grow?"

"Would you have run laps had your coach not required it? Would you have improved as an athlete had you not run the laps?" Messenger asked. "It is the way with mankind and the believer alike. The believer would settle into a comfortable, stagnant existence and not grow if it were not for tests and trials. God has the power and authority to prevent all trials for His children if He sees fit. But you must understand that God loves you more than you can imagine and His ultimate plan for you is for your own good. God knows all the tiniest details of your life. He knows and understands the pain you go through in your trials, for God the Son faced all those same trials when He lived in your world. But your loving Father will not exempt you from those trials, for He is growing you to Christ-likeness with those spiritual cycles, in which you apply His Word to your trial and experience His rescue or wisdom followed by His resting peace. These cycles are His training regimen by His design and for your spiritual growth. That is why trials and tests are necessary."

1. How does Messenger answer the question about the purpose of trials in the life of a follower of Christ? (Christ-likeness / to be like Christ. Discuss.)

2. Can you remember a recent trial that helped you grow closer to Christ? Can you now see that He had a plan for you through it? (Discuss) Close your session in Prayer.

SESSION FOUR

THE FEAST IN THE INNER CHAMBER

(COVERS JOURNEY BOOK CHAPTERS 10-11)

Read the following excerpt and discuss the questions that follow:

I watched Learner rise from the banquet table, where he had been eating. I followed him as he walked toward two large wooden doors that exited from the banquet hall. Over the large doors were inscribed these words: He Who Enters This Chamber Must Do So By Personal Abandonment and Absolute Trust. I watched Learner pause and read the words. I could tell he was considering the impact that such a commitment would have on his life. This was a serious, life-changing challenge, and it could not be entered into without considering the cost. I couldn't help but think he was remembering where he had come from, outside the Kingdom's walls, and his process of development since then. I thought, "He has to realize that the One Who has loved him and brought him this far would never ask anything of him that would hurt him or betray him even with the challenge that is being asked of him." After a while of contemplation, Learner nodded as if to assure himself of the things I had come to think. Then he opened the massive doors and walked into the Chamber. I was behind Learner as the doors opened, and I could see the contents of the Inner Chamber. The room was not big. It could even be described as cozy. The walls were richly paneled with beautiful woodwork. On the walls hung pieces of shining armor, swords and fighting equipment. On the far wall was a large stone fireplace with a blazing fire. Over the mantle was a large shield with the emblem of a lion and a lamb. The wood floor and the paneled walls reflected a soft, golden glow from the fire, which was the room's source of light. In front of the fireplace, two comfortable-looking overstuffed chairs faced each other. If not for the room's warmth, this could have been some kind of war room because of the armament on the walls.

This was no war room in a traditional sense, but one could sense that many battles had been prepared for in this room by the strategies that would have been discussed in those two chairs. I was eagerly moving to the entrance to follow Learner when Messenger blocked my way. "You cannot enter this time and place with Learner," he said. "It is reserved only for Learner." As he spoke, the massive doors began to close. "I will explain to you what is happening so you will know what to expect if you choose to enter the Feast in the Inner Chamber," Messenger stated. "Why could I not join Learner in the Chamber?" I asked. Messenger replied, "The Feast in the Inner Chamber is a private and deeply spiritual time for Learner. It is not to be observed, but experienced. You will understand this firsthand should you choose to go forward in your spiritual journey upon returning to your world.

1. The words **Personal Abandonment** and **Absolute Trust** frighten a lot of Christians. To think that releasing control of one's life and trusting Christ on a level such as this is a serious challenge to most people. How do you feel about it? (Discuss)

2. Most people would like to think that they have control of the important things in life such as their future, their "treasures," their health and their relationships. But how many of these things, or any thing that is not listed, do we have absolute control over? (Discuss)

Jim Elliot, a former missionary who was martyred by a primitive tribe in Ecuador in 1956, had written the following words in his journal shortly before being murdered:

> *"He is no fool who gives what he cannot keep to gain that which he cannot lose."* — *Jim Elliot*

3. What do you think Jim Elliot was referencing when he said he would risk that which he could not keep to gain that which he could not lose? (Discuss)

4. If Jim couldn't keep his life safe from those who murdered him, did God have the power and right to do so? Do you think Jim was willing to entrust his life to God, no matter the cost, because God did have control of it? (Discuss)

5. Do you think Jim's death was wasted, or was his life invested as God would choose, even if it meant his death? (Discuss)

Jim Elliot lost his life. But what was gained from this loss was a people who were once lost in sin, but were saved for eternity. Jim was used to gain eternal life for those who would never lose it once it was found. Was he a fool to risk control of that which he could not keep to gain eternal life for a lost people? Some would say yes. But for those who came to know Christ as a result, they would have a different opinion.

6. When Learner abandoned himself to Christ, and decided to trust Him absolutely, what was the result? He became equipped. He grew in courage. He was prepared to be an Influencer to his world around him. He became a dangerous warrior for Christ. Do you think he would have trusted Christ on this level without learning to self-feed, and getting to know Him better beforehand?

Read the following excerpt and discuss your answer afterwards:

Messenger paused before beginning his next statement: "You were expecting a continuation of the spiritual food that Learner was partaking of in the banquet hall. Therefore, you were surprised to see that there wasn't a banquet table waiting for him. Understand that everything Learner was partaking of in the banquet hall was leading him to the Feast in the Inner Chamber. All of the spiritual food he was taking in before going into the Chamber was making him hungrier for the Feast ahead. All the spiritual food was placing in him a desire for something beyond what he was experiencing. In the Chamber, Learner is finding what he has craved all his life. In the Chamber, Learner is partaking of the Feast that all mankind is starving for. The Feast that Learner is partaking of right now is the Lord God, Himself."

Messenger's words hit me like a ton of bricks. I was surprised that this was the meaning of the Feast in the Inner Chamber, but it made perfect sense. I could see how all of God's efforts have been to bring mankind back to Himself. I could see that He is not satisfied, nor should we be, with a beginning salvation experience. It is His purpose to draw us deeper and deeper into our relationship with Him. I could see that it is out of that deepening, intimate relationship that the supernatural is transferred to the ordinary. This was the message Jesus was giving us when He said we must abide in

Him and He in us. The transformation in the believer's life comes by this abiding with Him, and it is in this abiding fellowship that He imparts His characteristics and values. The Feast in the Inner Chamber is, in truth, the time we spend in this abiding fellowship with Christ. Yes, it all began to make sense.

7. Is it beginning to make sense to you what is missing in your life? If it frightens you to abandon yourself and to trust Christ absolutely, it may be because you have not come to know Him as you need to know Him, to trust him on that level. It may be because you have not yet learned first hand, that He is trustworthy. But, do you sincerely want to know the man or woman God can make of you?

8. If you were to be asked where you see yourself in the allegory you have just read, where would you say you are in Learner's journey? What do you think needs to be done about it? (Discuss)

Close your session in Prayer.

PART TWO

SESSION FIVE: **GABE**
(COVERS JOURNEY BOOK CHAPTERS 12-16)

SESSION SIX: **THE FRUIT THAT LASTS**
(COVERS JOURNEY BOOK CHAPTERS 17-20)

SESSION FIVE

GABE

(COVERS JOURNEY BOOK CHAPTERS 12-16)

"As the writer of this book I have come to understand how endearing Gabe is to many people who read about him. I have also seen this affection for the man expand to different cultures around the world through our translated material. We have been amazed that Gabe's influence is not limited to the culture he came from. Why is this? I think it is because he conveys through the purity of his faith and the characteristics of his life, the great influence someone can have simply by abiding with Christ, and that it is timeless and limitless with its application to our life. The concept that a humble man, in the most unlikely of circumstances, can still be a man of great influence is sound biblical theology, but it also goes against the grain of what our society believes about an "influential" person. After all, is it similar to the circumstances around Jesus when and where He lived? Remember what Nathanael asked about Jesus? (Nathanael said to him, "Can anything good come out of Nazareth?" John 1:46) Even Jesus, the most influential person who ever walked the earth was stereotyped as someone who could not be influential, because He didn't fit the mold. This is the way the world sees influence, but God

sees it differently. Gabe becomes an example to us that it is Christ in us who makes sure to use us for His purposes, and that our life is not wasted. In fact we become great influencers for Him. This example we see in Gabe then becomes an encouragement, even hope for all of us that we too can leave a spiritual legacy that will not end when we take our last breath, and we too can be of great influence to our world around us no matter our circumstances. Gabe's life gives us hope, for in it we see what we could also become if we will walk with Christ, and then allow God to use us according to His plan."
—Rocky Fleming

1. What characteristics in Gabe do you see that you admire the most? (Discuss)

2. Have you ever known a man or woman who you would say reminds you of Gabe? What is, or was, your relationship with this person, and how did he or she influence you? (Discuss)

3. As you consider the person, there were likely tests and trials that developed the character, the faith, the demeanor, and the influence in their life. Do you know of some of those trials they had to overcome to become the person they were/are? (Discuss)

4. In the story, we see a unique interaction with Gabe and the storyteller. Look at the dialogue in the excerpt included:

> *"I recounted my trip. I could tell that Gabe was interested as he grabbed hold of every word. I then asked if there was a motel or town nearby so I could get help and find a place to spend the night.*
>
> *Gabe answered, "There's a small town about 20 miles down the road and they have a wrecker service, but no one will be getting out in this weather. I don't have a telephone but when*

the storm stops I'll get out my truck and take you there. As far as a place to stay, you're welcome to stay here. Besides, there is no way we should get out in this storm tonight."

I thought about the offer and said, "I would hate to impose on your hospitality, but it appears that I don't have a choice. I'll be glad to pay you for your accommodations and inconvenience."

Gabe stood, walked to the stove and poured another cup of coffee as he shook his head. 'Son, I guess you haven't come to understand the joy someone can have by just being a blessing to someone in need. You've probably been living in such a dog-eat-dog world that to give a helping hand to someone in trouble is a sign of weakness or worse, you don't help for you think he brought it on himself. Now don't you worry about paying me for my inconvenience because I've been well paid for these services way before you ever walked in my door. You're my guest and it is my pleasure to help you.'"

1. Gabe had to take a risk to invite a stranger in need into his home in the night, didn't he? To do this, didn't he have to live with a sense of abandonment of his fears and to trust God on a deeper level? He mentioned that he had been well paid for his services before our storyteller ever walked into his house. What do you think Gabe meant by these words? (Discuss)

2. Do you think Gabe lived with a sense of gratitude toward God and that made him willing to serve this man like he did? Is that something needed in your own life? (Discuss)

3. Gabe took a great risk to invite a stranger into his house that night. It took courage. Where do you think this courage came from? Before answering the question, consider these words found in scripture:

"There is no fear in love, but perfect love casts out fear. For fear has to do with punishment, and whoever fears has not been perfected in love." 1 John 4:18 (ESV)

(Continued) There is only one perfect love and that is the love of God. How do God's love, and our abiding in it (being "perfected" in it) take away our fear and make us courageous like Gabe? (Discuss)

In the story and dialogue between Gabe and the storyteller, we see many points that are made. Examples of some points made are:

- We see wisdom being sought and wisdom being conveyed. (How does that happen?)

- We see wisdom that comes from experiences, even trials in a life that had to be overcome, but results in an insight that could be found in no other way. (Why is this?)

- We see God "set" things in motion to both teach and show a model in a man of what it means to see a humble man in humble circumstances who simply walks with Christ, but has great insight to teach and guide someone who does not fit within his circumstances. Does society need to see a man living his life like this? (Why?)

- We see an influence that is not of this world being conveyed in an unlikely person and his circumstances, and we just know it is Christ within him that is at work. (How does this example of humble faithfulness teach you to live your life?)

With these points in mind, and those that are not mentioned but stand out to you, use the remaining time in the session to discuss these and other points that mean the most to you. *Please limit your discussion in this session to those teaching points found before Chapter 19. We will cover that discussion in Session 6.*

After your discussion, close with prayer.

SESSION SIX

A FRUIT THAT LASTS

(COVERS JOURNEY BOOK CHAPTERS 17-20)

Look at Jesus' instructions to His disciples in the Gospel of John:

> *"You did not choose me, but I chose you and appointed you that you should go and bear fruit and that your fruit should abide, so that whatever you ask the Father in my name, he may give it to you."*
> *John 15:16 (ESV)*

The word "abide" also means "remain." It is significant that the fruit that Christians produce comes only by way of our abiding in Christ. Jesus taught this in John 15. Likewise, the fruit He speaks of in that chapter and which remains after our life has ended, continues to abide. How can this be? The answer is that this fruit continues to find its way into other people's lives and points them to Christ. We can call this our spiritual legacy, where the life we had when we once lived, continues to influence after we die. I believe the fruit, which remains, and is what Jesus refers to, is our spiritual legacy as Christians. Note Jesus' emphasis on choice and appointment. He chose us for this work, and He appointed us to our mission of bearing fruit. Therefore, it is evident that Jesus had in mind our spiritual legacy even when we took fledgling steps in our relationship with Him. It is His plan for us to come and find it and then help others find it.

In the book we read about Gabe's legacy, as we join his funeral. It becomes apparent that his influence did not end at his death, for the memories of his life and influence remained in the minds of the people that lived on. The following examples show how Gabe's influence continued:

- **The church.** Gabe helped reconstruct this church and it was where his funeral was held. Would Gabe have been considered an "up front" guy in that congregation, or more of a foundational part of it? Is his discreet position less important than others? Why or why not? (Discuss)

- **If Gabe was an essential part of his church, what influence of his do you think remained after his death?** What made his influence survive? (Discuss)

- **The Pastor.** Certainly the pastor would be a great example of how Gabe's life continued to influence him even after his death. In fact, the pastor shared something that a lot of people took away from the funeral. It was called: Gabe's Principles of Influence. Look at each principle and discuss them:

Gabe's Principles of Influence:

Be a God Seeker: Why would this principle be first on Gabe's priority list? Why should it be first on our list? What are some practical ways that we "seek God?" (Discuss)

Be a God Abider: We tend toward thinking that being a God Seeker and a God Abider are the same. In what ways are they the same and in what ways are they different? In your own words, what do you think it means to abide in Christ? (Discuss)

Live it Out: Gabe lived by his priorities. But his "life" priorities were driven by first being a God Seeker and a God Abider. How could this process Gabe lived by be our guide to help us discover how to "Live it Out" in our life? (Discuss)

- **The Farmer:** Like any man, Gabe had to overcome a lot of personal emotions, anger and hurt to bless the farmer who tried to burn his barn down. What would have happened if Gabe had given into his anger and sought revenge? How would his spiritual legacy have been compromised if he had done so? (Discuss)

- **Concerning you:** Have you ever regretted words or actions spoken in haste? How would Gabe's reaction to the test given to him require courage, trust, and commitment to standing firm? How would you having an action plan established prior to your test, help matters rather than saying or doing things you might regret? (Discuss)

- **Are there any other points you read that touched and taught you?** (Discuss)

In the Epilogue we read these words:

"There should be a point in every believer's life when he evaluates the progress he is making in his spiritual journey. The most accurate measurement comes not in his comparison with other people or his spiritual works, but in the intimacy with Jesus Christ that grows in his life."

The question you need to answer, now that you have completed this book review, is whether you have gotten to the point where you are ready to make serious progress in your spiritual journey. If so, your target must be to grow in your intimate, abiding relationship with Christ. The next step that will take you to this place that you seek is found in our nine-month discipleship process called The Journey. The book you have just read and reviewed has been written to give you a hunger for this process, and most of all, for the Feast that awaits you. We hope that you will now take your next step. God bless you on your journey in The Journey.

The Spiritual Progression of Man

The Refugee Camp (See Romans 8:19-23) This represents the spiritual condition of the world, with people who look good on the outside but are starving on the inside. There is spiritual warfare with demons constantly attacking.

The Appetizer Table (See Isaiah 29:13, Deuteronomy 12:29-32) This represents all the "religions" of the world, with false enlightenments. Most of these are man seeking to appease or please God, rather than God seeking an intimate relationship with man.

The Bridge (See Luke 23:32-43, John 14:6, John 10:9, Romans 10:6-9) This represents Jesus Christ, as the ONLY way to get into the Kingdom of Heaven. It is a personal act and surrender of the will of an individual to God by believing and receiving His Son, Jesus.

The Table of Sweets (See Jeremiah 26:2-3) This represents spiritual messages or teaching that withholds the whole truth of Scripture. Many of these are "feel-good" thoughts but they are not ushering believers into God's Word where they can feast and grow spiritually.

The Banquet Table (See John 1:1, John 6:54-55) This represents the undiluted Word of God. It starts with baby food and help is needed by Mentors, but over time, the goal is for individuals to become self-feeders on God's Word.

The Exercise Room (See James 1:2-4, Romans 5:1-5, 1 Peter 4: 12-14) This represents trials that will come into the life of a believer. These trials allow him to test all of the nourishment (theology) he has been getting from the Banquet Table to see if it is really true. "Experience trumps Theory!" Also, it is a place of refreshing rest after a trial has been withstood and overcome. All of this builds more of hunger for God.

The Inner Chamber (See Revelation 3:20, John 15) This represents an abiding intimacy with Christ. The spiritual progression the Learner had been experiencing led him to a deeper intimacy with Christ. This will lead to a fruitful life.

THE SPIRITUAL PR